Cesar Chavez

by James T. Hickey

Table of Contents

Who Was Cesar Chavez? 2

How Did Cesar Chavez
Help Field Workers? 6

How Do People Remember Cesar Today? 16

Glossary and Index 20

Who Was Cesar Chavez?

Cesar Chavez spent his life helping **migrant workers**. Many migrant workers in America were not treated well. They were not given fair wages for their work. They were often too poor to feed their families. Their children often had to work, too.

Cesar Chavez wanted migrant workers to be treated better. He fought for them to have more rights. He helped them find a better way of life. His work is still admired and remembered today.

3

Cesar was born on March 31, 1927. His family lived on a farm near Yuma, Arizona. When Cesar was ten, his parents lost their farm. The family moved to California and became migrant workers.

Cesar's family was very poor. His parents made a living by moving around the country. They picked fruits and vegetables all day in the hot sun. Cesar helped his parents in the fields.

◀ **Cesar left school after completing the eighth grade to work in a field like the one shown.**

? Did You Know?

THE GREAT DEPRESSION

During the 1920s and 1930s, life was very difficult in the United States. Jobs were hard to find, and many people were poor. Some people lost their homes. Many were hungry. Children had to work to help raise money for their families. This time period is known as the Great Depression.

How Did Cesar Chavez Help Field Workers?

When Cesar was older, he dreamed of one day helping migrant workers. He saw young children working in fields and wanted to make their lives better. The children were not given much food to eat. They did not go to school. They worked all day in the fields. They helped make money for their families, just as Cesar had done when he was a boy.

▲ Four young boys help their parents pick onions in California.

Cesar wanted to help all migrant workers. He wanted them to have enough food to eat. He wanted them to be able to go to the doctor when they were sick. He wanted children to go to school so they wouldn't have to work in the fields when they grew up.

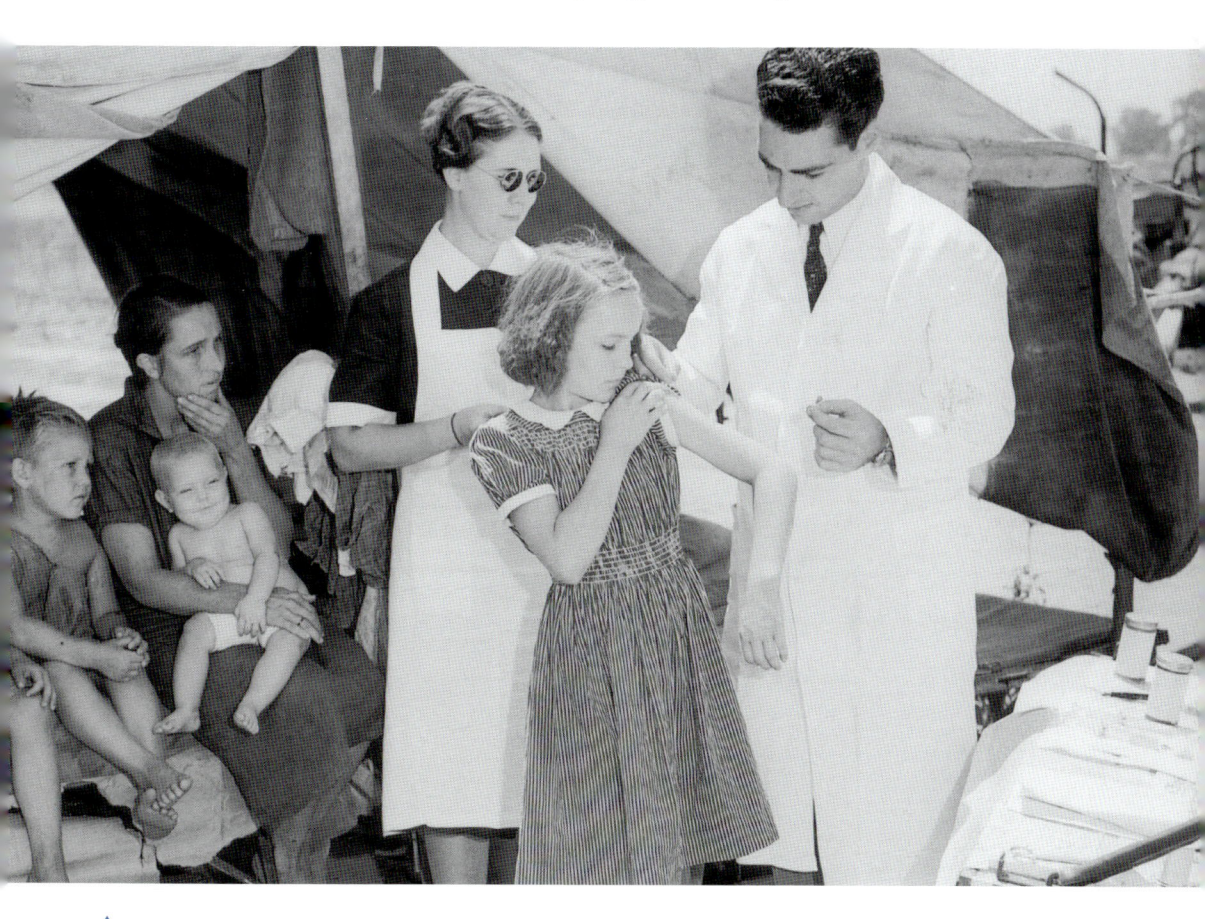

▲ A doctor gives medicine to children at a camp for migrant farm workers.

In the early 1960s, Cesar asked the farmers to pay their workers more money. The farmers refused. They wanted to keep all the money they earned from their farms.

Cesar got together as many workers as he could. He started a **union** of migrant workers called the United Farm Workers of America. This was the first successful union for farm workers.

The United Farm ▶
Workers of America
was formed in 1962.

Cesar told the workers to stop picking grapes until the farmers paid more money. He led the group in a **strike**. They refused to work until the farmers agreed to pay them better wages.

▲ Cesar helps organize a strike.

When the group stopped working in the fields, the farmers had a hard time finding other people to pick grapes. The farmers lost money because they did not have enough workers to pick the ripe grapes.

Cesar spoke out to the public. He told people how poor the field workers were. The news showed pictures of young children working all day in the hot sun. It showed children who were not getting enough food to eat. It showed pictures of sick children who needed to go to the doctor. Soon people started to listen.

All across the country, people started to feel sad for the farm workers. Many people agreed to a **boycott**. They stopped buying grapes. The farmers began to lose even more money. They saw that thousands of people thought the workers deserved better treatment. They learned how much they needed their field workers. The farmers agreed to pay and help their workers more.

Cesar Chavez led more than one grape boycott. In 1986 he squeezed these grapes to protest the use of harmful materials in the growing of grapes.

13

Cesar's hard work changed the lives of many people. Cesar was able to get better pay and better working conditions for field workers. He was able to get medical help for all the people who joined the United Farm Workers union, too.

15

How Do People Remember Cesar Today?

After years of hard work and dedication, Cesar died on April 23, 1993, at the age of sixty-six. Thousands of people came to his funeral to honor him.

After his death, Cesar was awarded the Presidential Medal of Freedom. This is the highest **civilian** award in the United States. It is given for public service.

In California, March 21 was made a state holiday to honor Cesar Chavez.

▲ the Presidential Medal of Freedom

Did You Know?

Other winners of the Presidential Medal of Freedom include Martin Luther King, Jr.; the astronauts Neil Armstrong and Buzz Aldrin; and John F. Kennedy.

Cesar's group is still working to help field workers and their families. They are keeping Cesar's dream alive.

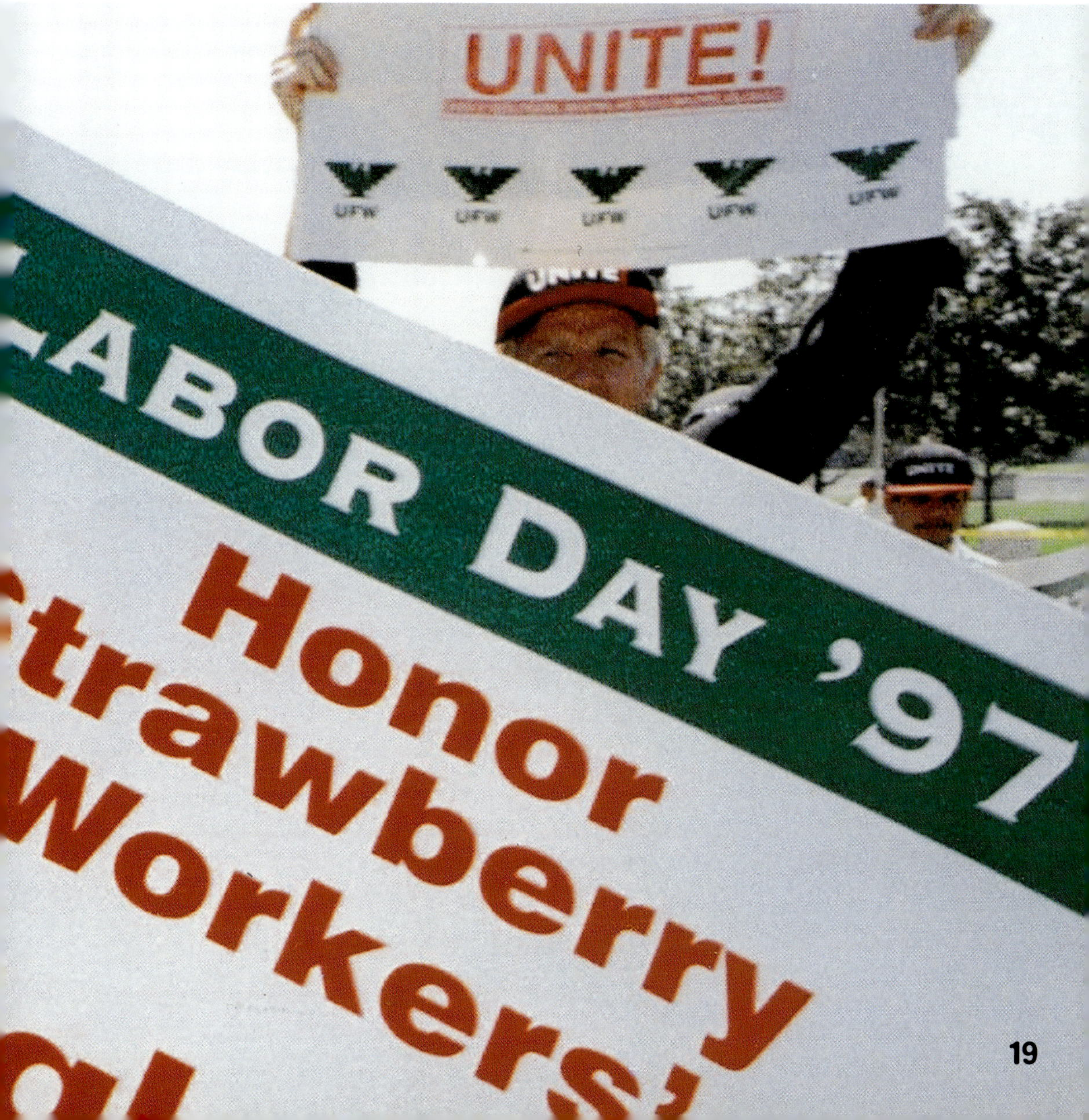
UNITE!
UFW
LABOR DAY '97
Honor
Strawberry
Workers'

Glossary

boycott (BOY-kaht): the refusal to buy or use certain products

Cesar Chavez (SEE-zer CHAH-vez): the founder of the United Farm Workers of America union

civilian (sih-VIL-yun): a person who is not part of the military

migrant workers (MY-grunt WER-kerz): people who travel to different areas to look for work

strike (STRIKE): the refusal to work until certain conditions are met

union (YOON-yun): a group that workers join to make sure they are treated fairly by the people they work for

Index

boycott 12	migrant workers 2, 4, 6–8
Cesar Chavez 2, 4–9, 11, 14, 16–18	strike 9
civilian 17	union 8, 14
field workers 4, 11–12, 14, 18	United Farm Workers of America 8, 14